STUDENT'S BOOK 3

SERIES EDITORS
Joan Kang Shin and
JoAnn (Jodi) Crandall

AUTHORS
Lesley Koustaff and
Susan Rivers

T0349576

1 **What can you hear at the beginning?**
Listen and circle. TR: 0.1

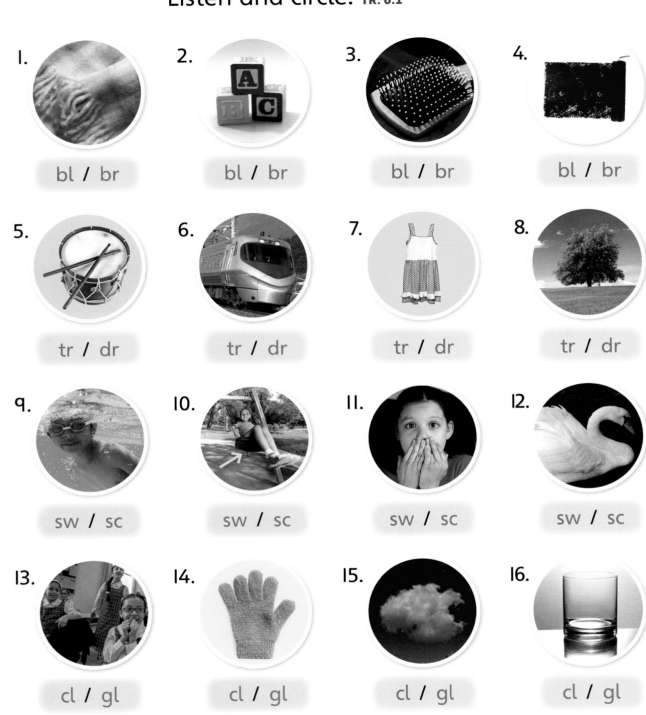

1. bl / br

2. bl / br

3. bl / br

4. bl / br

5. tr / dr

6. tr / dr

7. tr / dr

8. tr / dr

9. sw / sc

10. sw / sc

11. sw / sc

12. sw / sc

13. cl / gl

14. cl / gl

15. cl / gl

16. cl / gl

17. sl / fl

18. sl / fl

19. sl / fl

20. sl / fl

2 **Listen.** What can you hear at the beginning? Match. TR: 0.2

1.

cr

gr

2.

3.

sp

fr

4.

5.

sn

ch

6.

7.

gl

pr

8.

9.

st

sm

10.

11.

tr

sk

12.

3 **Which sounds can you hear?** Listen and write. TR: 0.3

| pl | fr | sn | pr | st |

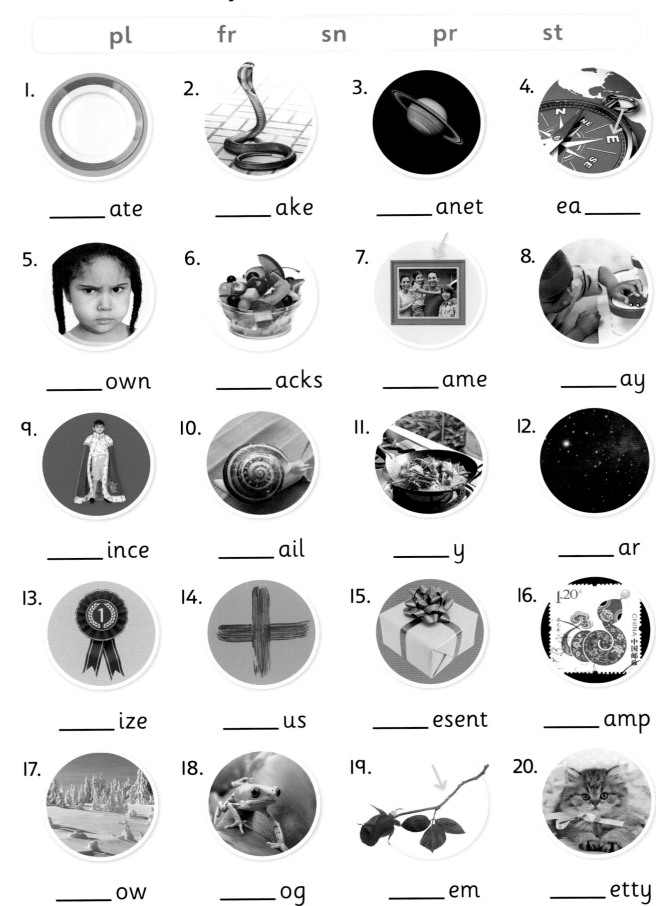

1. _____ate

2. _____ake

3. _____anet

4. ea_____

5. _____own

6. _____acks

7. _____ame

8. _____ay

9. _____ince

10. _____ail

11. _____y

12. _____ar

13. _____ize

14. _____us

15. _____esent

16. _____amp

17. _____ow

18. _____og

19. _____em

20. _____etty

4 **What words can you hear?** Listen and circle. TR: 0.4

1.	huge	hug	cube	cub
2.	talk	take	suit	sit
3.	coin	cone	plan	plane
4.	kite	coat	note	night
5.	mouse	moose	head	hide
6.	road	ride	hop	hope

5 **Which word is the odd one out?** Circle the word with a different vowel sound. Then listen to check your answers. TR: 0.5

1.	cry	bike	light	sit
2.	boy	home	soap	coat
3.	cake	bread	tail	day
4.	food	flute	fruit	good
5.	walk	sauce	cold	crawl

6 **What sound can you hear?** Listen and write. TR: 0.6

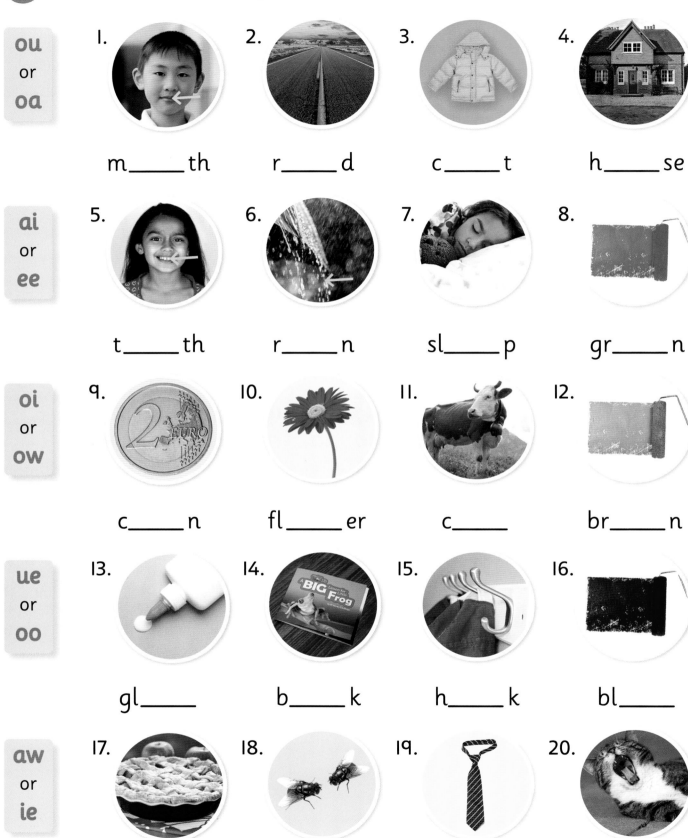

ou
or
oa

1. m_____th
2. r_____d
3. c_____t
4. h_____se

ai
or
ee

5. t_____th
6. r_____n
7. sl_____p
8. gr_____n

oi
or
ow

9. c_____n
10. fl_____er
11. c_____
12. br_____n

ue
or
oo

13. gl_____
14. b_____k
15. h_____k
16. bl_____

aw
or
ie

17. p_____
18. fl_____s
19. t_____
20. y_____n

7 **Follow the path to the words with the same vowel sound.** Then listen to check your answers. TR: 0.7

mouse   point   juice   read   phone

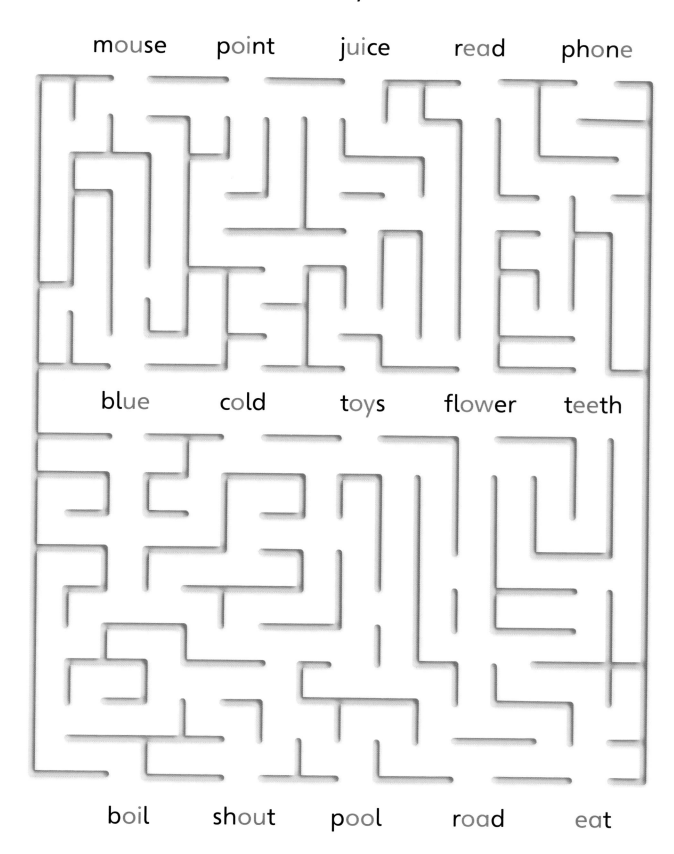

blue   cold   toys   flower   teeth

boil   shout   pool   road   eat

8 **Listen and repeat.** Write the word. TR: 0.8

1.

_____

2.

_____

3.

_____

4.

_____

5.

_____

6.

_____

7.

_____

8.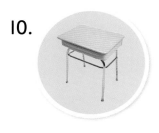

_____

9.

_____

10.

_____

11.

_____

12.

_____

13.

_____

14.

_____

15.

_____

16.

_____

17.

_____

18.

_____

19.

_____

20.

_____

9 **What word can you hear?** Listen and draw a line to make the word. TR: 0.9

1. br   t
       ea
   b   d

2. r   b
       a
   cr   p

3. cl   ve
       ea
   l   n

4. t   t
       ai
   b   l

5. b   k
       al
   w   l

6. sm   il
       a
   sn   ll

7. sh   f
       e
   ch   et

8. sn   ke
       a
   s   ck

9. br   s
       ow
   r   n

10. s   th
       o
    sl   ft

11. b   k
       oo
    br   ts

12. tr   m
        u
    dr   nk

13. sp   m
        i
    sl   n

14. pl   ne
        u
    pr   s

15. t   os
        o
    z   ys

16. m   se
        ou
    h   nt

17. t   be
        u
    c   b

18. c   ck
        a
    p   ke

19. n   ise
        o
    p   se

20. pr   n
        aw
    y   ns

1 syllable

pie

blue

2 syllables

tea•cher

win•dow

rain

frog

ap•ples

chil•dren

1 syllable

cheese

swim

2 syllables

dra•gon

bed•room

3 syllables

um•brel•la

tri•an•gle

11 **Listen and match.** TR: 0.11

grandmother

today

dress

hungry

I.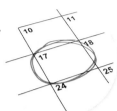

2.

3.

4.

1
syllable

2
syllables

3
syllables

5.

6.

7.

8.

kangaroo

plant

goodbye

cube

12 **Listen.** Which syllable is stressed? Circle. TR: 0.12

I.

me•cha•nic

2.

an•gry

3.

sand•wi•ches

4.

snow•flake

5.

win•dow

6.

con•trol•ler

11

1 **Listen.** Then listen and repeat. TR: 1.1 and 1.2

a

1.

2.

past**a**   b**a**lloon

e

1.

2.

kitch**e**n   cam**e**l

2 **Trace and say.**

3 **Listen.** Circle the words with a/e in the <u>underlined</u> syllable. TR: 1.3

1.

sa•<u>lad</u>

2.

<u>ba</u>•by

3.

break•<u>fast</u>

4.

pre•<u>sent</u>

4 **Where can you hear a/e?** Listen and repeat. Circle the syllable with a/e. TR: 1.4

a•gain   plea•sant   tra•vel   pan•da

5 **Listen.** Then listen and repeat. TR: 1.5 and 1.6

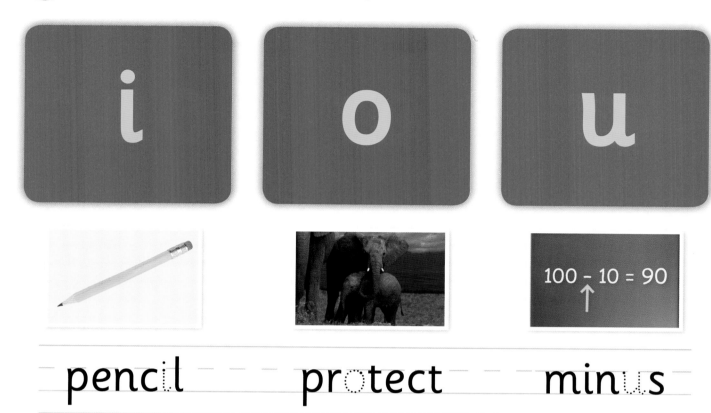

pencil   protect   minus

6 **Trace and say.**

7 **Listen.** Circle the words with i/o/u in the <u>underlined</u> syllable. TR: 1.7

1. blos•<u>som</u>   2. of•<u>fice</u>   3. cir•<u>cus</u>   4. <u>win</u>•dow

8 **Where can you hear i/o/u?** Listen and repeat. Circle the syllable with i/o/u. TR: 1.8

pi•lot   bot•tom   fos•sil   vi•rus

9 **Listen.** Then listen and repeat. TR: 1.9 and 1.10

sister   doctor   colour

10 **Trace and say.**

11 **Can you hear a word with er/or/our?** Listen and put a ✔ or a ✗. TR: 1.11

1. ☐   2. ☐   3. ☐   4. ☐

12 **Listen and repeat.** Put the letters in order to make words. TR: 1.12

1.    2.    3.    4.

_____   _____   _____   _____
ebtutr   rctraot   broaurh   nraebn

13 **Listen.** Then listen and repeat. TR: 1.13 and 1.14

ch air   h are   p ear

14 **Trace and say.**

15 **Can you hear the word with air/are/ear one or two times?** Listen and circle *1* or *2*. TR: 1.15

1. air 1 2   2. air 1 2   3. ear 1 2   4. are 1 2

16 **Which words rhyme with *chair*?** Listen and circle. TR: 1.16

1.    2.    3.    4.

bear   hair   heart   share

17 **Find and circle the words.** Then listen and repeat to check. TR: 1.17

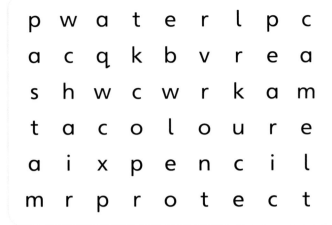

p w a t e r l p c
a c q k b v r e a
s h w c w r k a m
t a c o l o u r e
a i x p e n c i l
m r p r o t e c t

18 **Listen.** Then listen and chant. TR: 1.18

My mum and dad take care of me.
They're as busy as can be.
My mum and dad take care of me.
We're a happy family.

My parents protect our family,
my brother, my sister and me.
They teach us to share and also to care,
and they also look after our big dog, Bear.

My mum and dad take care of me.
They're as busy as can be.
My mum and dad take care of me.
We're a happy family.

Listen. Then listen and repeat. TR: 1.19 and 1.20

Angelo's Parrot

Angelo loves animals. His father gives him a parrot.

"Take care of Pia! Protect her!"

Pia's cage is by the table and chairs. Angelo gets newspaper for the bottom of the cage.

"Hello!"

"What? Is that my brother?"

Angelo has got some banana, pear, carrot and water.

"Banana!"

"What? Is that my sister?"

Angelo has got a surprise for Pia. It's a toy.

"Thanks!"

"Pia! You can talk!"

20 **Listen and write the words.** Then go to page 78. TR: 1.21

1. __ __ __ __ __
   2

2. __ __ __ __ __ __
      12

3. __ __ __ __ __
  7 9

4. __ __ __ __
     15

1 **Listen.** Then listen and repeat. TR: 2.1 and 2.2

ar

1.

   arm

2.

   park

3.

4.

5.

large   car   market

2 **Trace and say.**

3 **Can you hear a word with ar?** Listen and put a ✔ or a ✘. TR: 2.3

1. ☐   2. ☐   3. ☐   4. ☐

4 **Listen and repeat each word with ar.** Write the words. TR: 2.4

1.    2.    3.    4.

__ __ __ __   __ __ __   __ __ __ __

5 **Listen.** Then listen and repeat. TR: 2.5 and 2.6

or

1.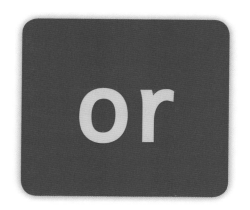
2.

horse   horn

3.
4.
5.

fork   corner   morning

6 **Trace and say.**

7 **Can you hear a word with or?** Listen and put a ✔ or a ✗. TR: 2.7

1. ☐   2. ☐   3. ☐   4. ☐

8 **Can you hear a word with or or ar?** Listen and write. TR: 2.8

1.
2.
3.
4.

sh____ts   ____tist   sp____t   b____n

19

9 **Listen.** Then listen and repeat. TR: 2.9 and 2.10

ear

1.

2.

ear   tear

eer

1.

2.

deer   cheer

10 **Trace and say.**

11 **Which words have got the ear/eer sound?** Listen and circle. TR: 2.11

1.    2.    3.    4.

12 **Does each pair of words rhyme?** Listen and circle *Yes* or *No*. TR: 2.12

1. Yes   No   2. Yes   No   3. Yes   No   4. Yes   No

13 **Listen.** Then listen and repeat. TR: 2.13 and 2.14

 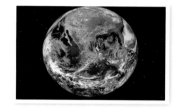 

shirt   Earth   nervous

14 **Trace and say.**

15 **Can you hear a word with ir/ear/er?** Listen and put a ✔ or a ✘. TR: 2.15

I. ☐   2. ☐   3. ☐   4. ☐

16 **Can you hear a word with ir or or?** Listen and write. TR: 2.16

I.    2.    3.    4.

g____l   d____t   b____d   c____n

17 **Write the words.** Then listen and check. TR: 2.17

1   2   3   4   5

18 **Listen.** Then listen and chant. TR: 2.18

We live in a small town.
We ride our horses all around.
You can see on my face.
This is my favourite place!

Our garden is like a park.
We can see deer near the trees.
We ride horses to the shop,
'Juice for thirsty girls, please!'

We live in a small town.
We ride our horses all around.
You can see on my face.
This is my favourite place!

19 **Listen.** Then listen and repeat. TR: 2.19 and 2.20

Fernanda's Surprise

It's a sunny morning in March. It's Fernanda's birthday.

They're in the car. They pass some horses.

They drive far. They see a deer. Mum honks her horn.

Surprise! There's a party for Fernanda at a park! She hears everyone cheer.

20 **Listen and write the words.** Then go to page 78. TR: 2.21

1. __ __ __
   11

2. __ __ __
   6 2

3. __ __ __ __ __ __
   16

4. __ __ __
   9

1 **Listen.** Then listen and repeat. TR: 3.1 and 3.2

1.

2.

n u r s e   t u r t l e

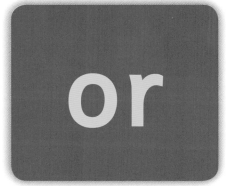

1.

2.

w o r l d   w o r k

2 **Trace and say.**

3 **Can you hear the word with ur/or one or two times?**
Listen and circle *1* or *2*. TR: 3.3

1. ur I 2   2. ur I 2   3. ur I 2   4. or I 2

4 **Have the two words got an ur/or sound?** Listen and
repeat. Circle *Yes* or *No*. TR: 3.4

1.    2.    3.    4.

Yes No   Yes No   Yes No   Yes No

5 **Listen.** Then listen and repeat. TR: 3.5 and 3.6

1.
4

f o u r

2.

p o u r

1.

d o o r

2.

fl o o r

6 **Trace and say.**

7 **Can you hear the word with our/oor one or two times?** Listen and circle *1* or *2*. TR: 3.7

1. our 1 2   2. oor 1 2   3. oor 1 2   4. our 1 2

8 **Can you hear a word with our or ur?** Listen and write. TR: 3.8

1.

y_____

2.

b_____ger

3.

c_____t

4.

c_____ly

9 **Listen.** Then listen and repeat. TR: 3.9 and 3.10

ire

1.

vamp**ire** bat

2.

3.

4.

f**ire**   w**ire**   t**ire**d

10 **Trace and say.**

11 **Have the two words got an ire sound?** Listen and repeat. Circle *Yes* or *No*. TR: 3.11

1. Yes   No   2. Yes   No   3. Yes   No   4. Yes   No

12 **Can you hear ire or ur?** Listen and write. TR: 3.12

1.

2.

3.

4.

f____works   ump_____   t____tle   c___tain

26

13 **Listen.** Then listen and repeat. TR: 3.13 and 3.14

our

1.

s our

2.

fl our

ower

1.

sh ower

2.

fl ower

14 **Trace and say.**

15 **Can you hear the word with our/ower one or two times?** Listen and circle *1* or *2*. TR: 3.15

1. ower 1 2   2. our 1 2   3. our 1 2   4. our 1 2

16 **Listen and repeat.** Put the letters in order to make words. TR: 3.16

1.

_____
orhu

2.

_____
oetwr

3.

_____
eodrvu

4.

_____
ropew

17 **Write the missing letters.** Follow the path to the words with the same sound. Then listen and check. TR: 3.17

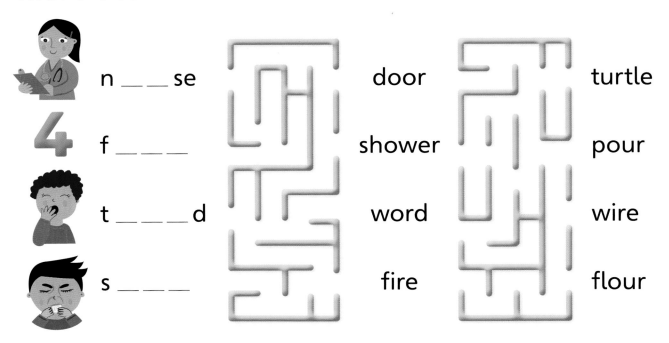

n _ _ se

f _ _ _ _

t _ _ _ d

s _ _ _ _

door

shower

word

fire

turtle

pour

wire

flour

18 **Listen.** Then listen and chant. TR: 3.18

*My family works hard every day
off to work by car and by train.*

*My mum is a nurse.
She loves her work.
My dad plants flowers
in the sun for hours.
They come back at four.
I'm always at the door.
We have dinner
and sit by the fire.*

*My family works hard every day
off to work by car and by train.*

Listen. Then listen and repeat. TR: 3.19 and 3.20

Fireworks!

20 **Listen and write the words.** Then go to page 78. TR: 3.21

1. __ __ __ __ __ __
   6

2. __ __ __ __ __ __
   16

3. __ __ __ __
   2 12

4. __ __ __ __
   13   8

Start

aptsa

p_____

hicar

c_____

aerp

p_____

4

Move forwards I space.

eicpln

p_____

Move
back
1 space.

thsri

s _____

ered

d _____

Finish

lfewor

f _____

otdroc

d _____

1 **Work in pairs.** Write the words.

2 **Play the game.** Spell and
say the words.

n-u-r-s-e,
nurse

Heads:
Move
1 space.

Tails:
Move
2 spaces.

31

1 **Listen.** Then listen and repeat. TR: 4.1 and 4.2

s   **s**   **es**

eats   reads   watches

2 **Trace and say.**

3 **Can you hear the same *s* sound at the end?** Listen and circle *Yes* or *No*. TR: 4.3

1. Yes No   2. Yes No   3. Yes No   4. Yes No

4 **Can you hear s as in *eats*, s as in *reads* or es as in *watches*?** Listen and circle green, blue or black. TR: 4.4

1.
tastes

2.
hugs

3.
washes

4.
smiles

5 **Listen.** Then listen and repeat. **TR: 4.5 and 4.6**

ful

1.

2.

beauti**ful**   aw**ful**

ous

1.

2.

delici**ous** nutriti**ous**

6 **Trace and say.**

7 **Can you hear ful or ous?** Listen and write. **TR: 4.7**

1. enorm_____   2. grate_____   3. jeal_____   4. colour_____

8 **Listen and repeat.** Put the letters in order to make words. **TR: 4.8**

1.

2.

3.

4.

_____   _____   _____   _____
esvunro   epuhfll   uafosm   lpyaluf

9 **Listen.** Then listen and repeat. TR: 4.9 and 4.10

1.

2.

qu**een**   qu**estion**

1.

2.

squ**are**   squ**irrel**

10 **Trace and say.**

11 **Can you hear qu or squ?** Listen and write. TR: 4.11

1. li____id   2. ____iet   3. _____int   4. _____ash

12 **Listen and repeat.** Put the letters in order to make words. TR: 4.12

1.    2.    3.    4.

_____   _____   _____   _____

uzqi   qsdiu   iukcq   qsriut

13 **Listen.** Then listen and repeat. TR: 4.13 and 4.14

fork   dolphin   laugh

14 **Trace and say.**

15 **Can you hear f/ph/gh at the beginning, in the middle or at the end?** Listen and repeat. Tick. TR: 4.15

1. ph ◯ ◯ ◯   2. f ◯ ◯ ◯   3. gh ◯ ◯ ◯   4. f ◯ ◯ ◯

16 **Listen and repeat.** Put the letters in order to make words. TR: 4.16

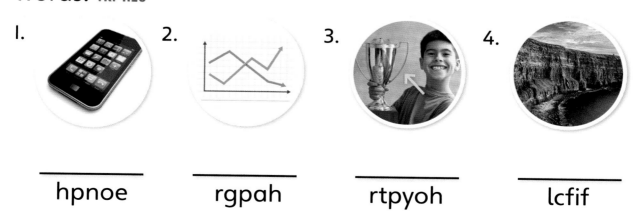

1. _____   2. _____   3. _____   4. _____

hpnoe   rgpah   rtpyoh   lcfif

17 **Find and circle the words.** Then listen and repeat
to check. TR: 4.17

c	b	e	a	u	t	i	f	u	l	s
q	i	t	a	s	t	e	s	f	a	m
u	q	v	w	r	c	y	z	o	u	i
e	s	b	q	x	t	p	k	r	g	l
e	n	s	q	u	a	r	e	k	h	e
n	u	t	r	i	t	i	o	u	s	s

18 **Listen.** Then listen and chant. TR: 4.18

I love to have fun outside.
The world is amazing to me.
I love to sit and look around
as far as my eyes can see.

This apple smells and tastes so good.
That squirrel is quick and quiet.
I'm grateful for the buzzing bees
that make delicious honey.
Funny selfies make me laugh.
Come and take some photos with me!

I love to have fun outside.
The world is amazing to me.
I love to sit and look around
as far as my eyes can see.

Listen. Then listen and repeat. TR: 4.19 and 4.20

Stephen's Cake!

Stephen wants to make a cake. He needs eggs, flour, sugar and squash.

Wonderful!

He stirs everything together. Then he pours it into a square tin. It smells delicious.

Mmm!

It bakes quickly. Stephen takes a photo. He phones Felicia.

Come over for cake!

Stephen gives Felicia an enormous piece and a fork.

It tastes really salty. It's awful!

Oh, no! It was salt, not sugar!

20 **Listen and write the words.** Then go to page 79. TR: 4.21

1. __ __ __ __ __ __
   17 3

2. __ __ __ __ __
            4 1

3. __ __ __ __ __
   8 18

4. __ __ __ __ __
         12

1 Listen. Then listen and repeat. TR: 5.1 and 5.2

nd

nk

nt

wetland   trunk   plant

2 Trace and say.

3 Can you hear the sound at the end one or two times?
Listen and circle *1* or *2*. TR: 5.3

1. nd 1 2   2. nk 1 2   3. nt 1 2   4. nt 1 2

4 Can you hear nd, nk or nt? Listen and write. TR: 5.4

1.

2.

3.

4.

te____   poi____   ha____   chipmu____

5 **Listen.** Then listen and repeat. TR: 5.5 and 5.6

I.    2.

goat   kangaroo

I.    2.

giraffe   large

6 **Trace and say.**

7 **Can you hear g as in *goat* or g as in *giraffe*?** Listen and circle green or blue. TR: 5.7

I.    2.    3.    4.

goose   orange   mug   vegetables

8 **What words with g can you hear?** Listen and write. TR: 5.8

I. _____   2. _____   3. _____   4. _____

9 **Listen.** Then listen and repeat. TR: 5.9 and 5.10

1.

bri d ge

2.

e d ge

1.

r h ino

2.

w h ite

10 **Trace and say.**

11 **Listen.** Circle the words with a silent *d* or silent *h*. TR: 5.11

1. Wednesday   2. body   3. honest   4. heart

12 **Listen and repeat.** Put the letters in order to make words. TR: 5.12

1.

_____
abgde

2.

_____
hsgot

3.

_____
hsewpri

4.

_____
idrfge

40

13 **Listen.** Then listen and repeat. **TR: 5.13 and 5.14**

nch

1.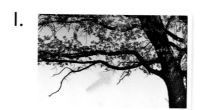

branch

2.

lunch

rch

1.

march

2.

search

14 **Trace and say.**

15 **Can you hear a word with nch or rch?** Listen and circle. **TR: 5.15**

1. nch / rch   2. nch / rch   3. nch / rch   4. nch / rch

16 **Can you hear nch or rch?** Listen and write. **TR: 5.16**

1.

be_____

2.

a_____

3.

to_____

4.

bu_____

17 **Write the words.** Complete the sentence with the hidden word. Then listen and check. TR: 5.17

Wild _____ live in mountains.

18 **Listen.** Then listen and chant. TR: 5.18

Animals are amazing.
Watch what they do
to eat and drink,
and to play, too!

Elephants bend their trunks
to eat and drink all day.
Giraffes munch on leaves
they get from tall trees.
Rhinos with their handsome horns
are giant vegetarians.

Animals are amazing.
Watch what they do
to eat and drink,
and to play, too!

19 **Listen.** Then listen and repeat. TR: 5.19 and 5.20

Camping with Aunt Giada

Aunt Giada, Gaia, Belinda and Bella go camping. They search for animals.

A chipmunk!

A hedgehog!

The girls get branches for the fire. They munch on sandwiches and listen to stories.

Then, a large bear...

The girls are in their tent. They hear a noise. They whisper.

It's huge!

It's a bear!

The girls peek out. They giggle.

It's Bella!

Bella has got a new friend. It's a frog!

20 **Listen and write the words.** Then go to page 79. TR: 5.21

l. __ __ __ __ __ __ __
    5 15

2. __ __ __ __ __ __
    13

3. __ __ __ __ __
    9 6

4. __ __ __ __
    8

1 **Listen.** Then listen and repeat. TR: 6.1 and 6.2

ble **dle** **ple**

ta_ble_   noo_dle_   ap_ple_

2 **Trace and say.**

3 **What word can you hear?** Listen and write the order
1–4. TR: 6.3

☐ candle   ☐ cable   ☐ couple   ☐ cuddle

4 **Can you hear ble, dle or ple?** Listen and write. TR: 6.4

1.    2.    3.    4.

pur____   pud____   han____   mar____

5 **Listen.** Then listen and repeat. TR: 6.5 and 6.6

cir**cle**   jun**gle**   bot**tle**

6 **Trace and say.**

7 **What word can you hear?** Listen and write the order 1–4. TR: 6.7

☐ beetle ☐ beagle ☐ bicycle ☐ bugle

8 **Can you hear cle, gle or tle?** Listen and write. TR: 6.8

1.  2.  3.  4.

ea_____   trian_____   ket_____   recy_____

9 Listen. Then listen and repeat. TR: 6.9 and 6.10

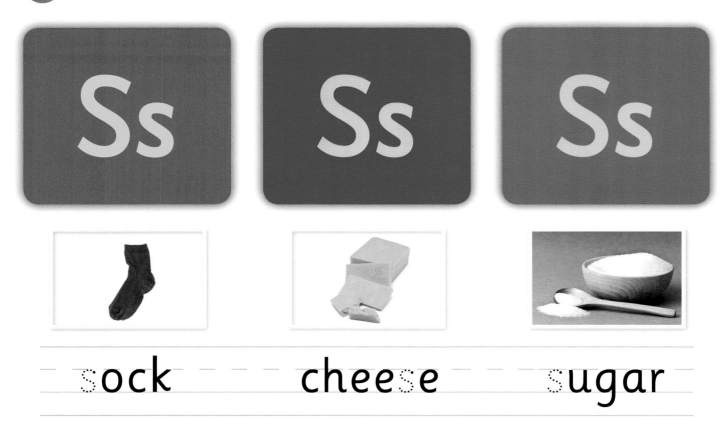

sock   cheese   sugar

10 Trace and say.

11 Listen. Circle the words with s as in *cheese*. TR: 6.11

1. lose   2. loss   3. bus   4. busy

12 Can you hear s as in *sock*, s as in *cheese* or s as in *sugar*? Listen and circle green, blue or black. TR: 6.12

1. tissue   2. pasta   3. music   4. nose

13 **Listen.** Then listen and repeat. TR: 6.13 and 6.14

1.

cake

2.

doctor

1.

cereal

2.

rice

14 **Trace and say.**

15 **What word can you hear?** Listen and write the order 1–4. TR: 6.15

☐ code   ☐ centre   ☐ cabin   ☐ mice

16 **Can you hear c as in *cake* or c as in *cereal*?** Listen and circle green or blue. TR: 6.16

1.

spice

2.

celery

3.

carrot

4.

calf

17 Write the missing letter. Follow the path to the words with the same letter and sound. Then listen and check.

TR: 6.17

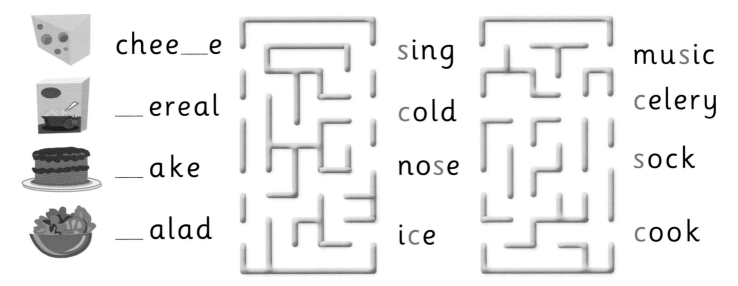

chee__e   sing   music

__ereal   cold   celery

__ake   nose   sock

__alad   ice   cook

18 Listen. Then listen and chant. TR: 6.18

Dinner with our family
is the best time of the day.
It's time to eat!
Hip, hip hooray!

Our uncle's noodles are tasty.
A little more, please.
Grandma's rice tastes great
with carrots and peas.
Purple bubbles in my drink
tickle my nose.
Dad's sugary desserts are the best
as everyone knows.

Dinner with our family
is the best time of the day.
It's time to eat!
Hip, hip hooray!

Listen. Then listen and repeat. TR: 6.19 and 6.20

Try a Little, Cesar!

Cesar only eats cereal. He won't eat noodles, apples, scrambled eggs or salad.

There's always trouble at the kitchen table. Uncle Carlos has got an idea.

Carlos gives Cesar some cheese, olives and biscuits. He likes them all!

Cesar likes all the food. He giggles.

20 **Listen and write the words.** Then go to page 79. TR: 6.21

1. __ __ __ __ __ __ __
    4   7

2. __ __ __ __ __ __
      17

3. __ __ __ __ __ __ __
    I

4. __ __ __ __ __
    II

Review

1 **Write the letters.**

s	ful	qu	squ	ph	gh	nk	g
h	rch	nch	ble	tle	s	c	c

ta_____

bra_____

taste_____

sea_____

lau_____

r_____ino

beauti_____

bot_____

tru_____

do_____tor

_____een

ri_____e

kan_____aroo

dol_____in

_____irrel

chee_____e

2 **Write the words in the grid in pencil.** Use a different word order.

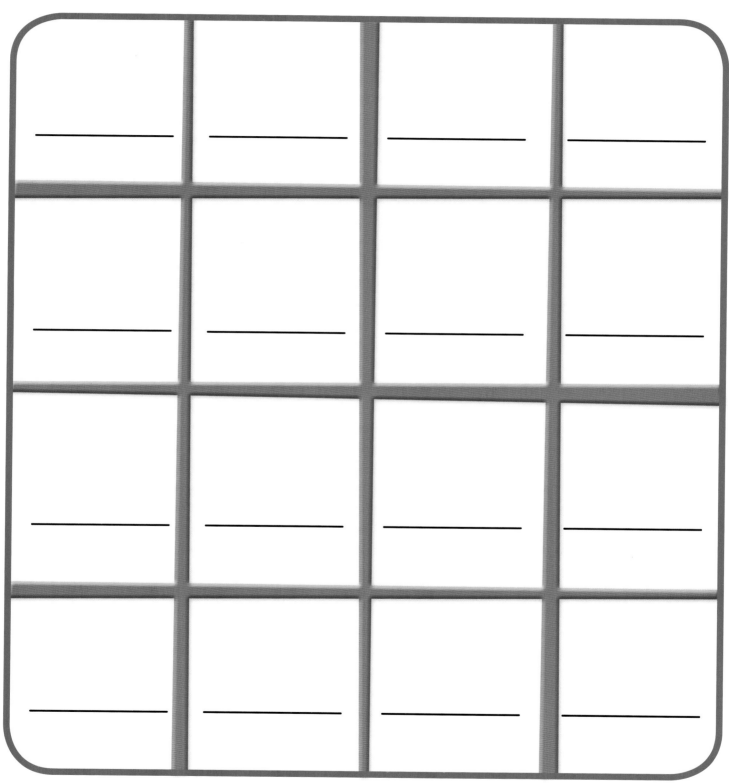

3 **Play *BINGO!*** Tick ✔ the words as you hear them.

1 **Listen.** Then listen and repeat. TR: 7.1 and 7.2

spr

spl

1.

spr**ing**

2.

spr**ead**

1.

spl**ash**

2.

spl**int**

2 **Trace and say.**

3 **Can you hear a word with spr or spl?** Listen and write the order 1–4. TR: 7.3

spr ☐☐

spl ☐☐

4 **Can you hear spr or spl?** Listen and write. TR: 7.4

1.

_____out

2.

_____its

3.

_____inkles

4.

_____inkler

5 Listen. Then listen and repeat. TR: 7.5 and 7.6

str

1.

2.

str**eet**   str**ing**

scr

1.

2.

scr**ew**   scr**een**

6 Trace and say.

7 Can you hear a word with str or scr? Listen and write the order 1–4. TR: 7.7

str ☐ ☐   scr ☐ ☐

8 Can you hear str or scr? Listen and write. TR: 7.8

1.

2.

3.

4.

_____aw   _____atch   _____eam   _____etch

9 **Listen.** Then listen and repeat. TR: 7.9 and 7.10

1.

shrimp

2.

shred

1.

throw

2.

three

10 **Trace and say.**

11 **Can you hear a word with shr or thr?** Listen and circle. TR: 7.11

1. shr / thr   2. shr / thr   3. shr / thr   4. shr / thr

12 **Can you hear shr or thr?** Listen and write. TR: 7.12

1.

2.

3.

4.

____ink   ____oat   ____ug   ____one

13 **Listen.** Then listen and repeat. TR: 7.13 and 7.14

silent k

1.

knee

2.

knock

silent t

1.

listen

2.

kitchen

14 **Trace and say.**

15 **Listen.** Circle the words with silent *k* or silent *t*. TR: 7.15

1. know   2. itch   3. king   4. light

16 **Listen and repeat.** Then put the letters in order to make words. TR: 7.16

1.
_____
nkto

2.
_____
ahmct

3.
_____
ntki

4.
_____
atcesl

17 **Find and circle the words.** Then listen and repeat to check. TR: 7.17

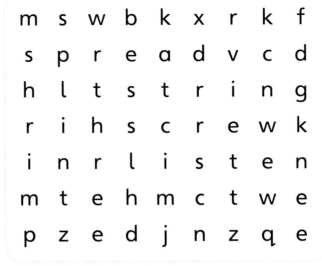

```
m  s  w  b  k  x  r  k  f
s  p  r  e  a  d  v  c  d
h  l  t  s  t  r  i  n  g
r  i  h  s  c  r  e  w  k
i  n  r  l  i  s  t  e  n
m  t  e  h  m  c  t  w  e
p  z  e  d  j  n  z  q  e
```

18 **Listen.** Then listen and chant. TR: 7.18

Be healthy and keep fit.
It's important to do.
Eat well and exercise.
It's good for you.

Splash around in a pool. Run sprints all day long.
Stretch your whole body and try to stay strong.
Throw a ball 1, 2, 3 and bend your knees.
Don't shrug your shoulders.
Jump over boulders!

Be healthy and keep fit.
It's important to do.
Eat well and exercise.
It's good for you.

19 Listen. Then listen and repeat. **TR: 7.19 and 7.20**

Why Can't Mitch Play?

20 Listen and write the words. Then go to page 80. **TR: 7.21**

1. __ __ __ __ __
   9   6

2. __ __ __ __
   15

3. __ __ __ __ __
   11

4. __ __ __ __ __ __
   1   17

1 **Listen.** Then listen and repeat. TR: 8.1 and 8.2

tion

1.

2.

invita<u>tion</u> decora<u>tion</u>s

sion

1.

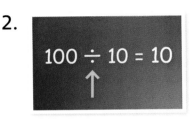

2.

$100 \div 10 = 10$

televi<u>sion</u>   divi<u>sion</u>

2 **Trace and say.**

3 **Can you hear a word with tion or sion?** Listen and write the number. TR: 8.3

tion ☐ ☐   sion ☐ ☐

4 **Can you hear a word with tion or sion?** Listen and write. TR: 8.4

1.

sta_____

2.

colli_____

3.
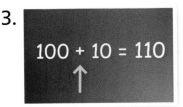
$100 + 10 = 110$
addi_____

4.

lo_____

58

5 **Listen to the words about the past.** Then listen and repeat. TR: 8.5 and 8.6

1.

2.

play*ed*   listen*ed*

1.

2.

danc*ed*   walk*ed*

6 **Trace and say.**

7 **Listen.** Circle the words with ed as in *played*. TR: 8.7

1. liked   2. rained   3. smiled   4. brushed

8 **Can you hear a word with ed as in *played* or ed as in *danced*?** Listen and circle green or blue. TR: 8.8

1.
coloured

2.
jumped

3.
climbed

4.
laughed

9 **Listen to the words about the past.** Then listen and repeat. TR: 8.9 and 8.10

1.

2.

visited   waited

3.

4.

5.

painted   folded   added

10 **Trace and say.**

11 **Listen.** Circle the words with ed as in *visited*. TR: 8.11

1. knitted   2. asked   3. landed   4. called

12 **Can you hear ed as in *played*, ed as in *danced* or ed as in *visited*?** Listen and circle green, blue or black. TR: 8.12

1.

2.

3.

4.

pointed   cooked   hugged   protected

13 **Listen.** Then listen and repeat. **TR: 8.13 and 8.14**

mother   birthday   spider

14 **Trace and say.**

15 **Can you hear the word with the sound one or two times?** Listen and circle *1* or *2*. **TR: 8.15**

1. d 1 2   2. th 1 2   3. d 1 2   4. th 1 2

16 **Listen and repeat.** Write *th* or *d*. **TR: 8.16**

1.    2.    3.    4.

para___e   ma_____s   clou_____y   fea_____er

17 **Write the words.** Complete the sentence with the hidden word. Then listen and check. TR: 8.17

1   2   3

4   5

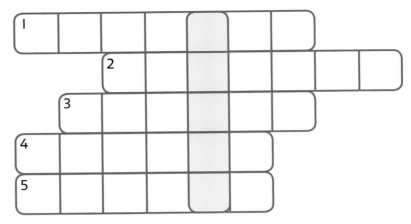

1							

They _____ a cake for the celebration.

18 **Listen.** Then listen and chant. TR: 8.18

Celebrations are fun,
so come on everyone.
Celebrate with us all day.
Dance and sing and play.

We enjoyed the celebration,
and put up decorations.
We danced and played
and walked in a parade.
We waited until dark
for the fireworks to start.
We all loved the show,
especially my brother, Joe.

Celebrations are fun,
so come on everyone.
Celebrate with us all day.
Dance and sing and play.

19 **Listen.** Then listen and repeat. TR: 8.19 and 8.20

A Birthday Celebration

Last week it was Daiyu's brother's birthday. She made a big decision.

Let's have a celebration!

She texted invitations. She coloured decorations. She baked a cake. She wrapped presents.

HAPPY BiRthday

Everyone arrived at three o'clock. They played games and danced. Then they all wanted cake.

Oh, no! Where's Daiyu?

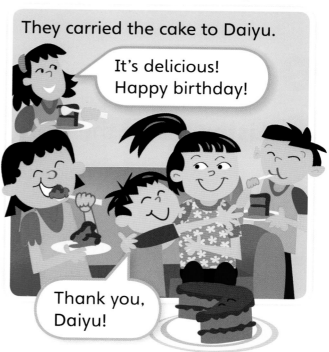

They carried the cake to Daiyu.

It's delicious! Happy birthday!

Thank you, Daiyu!

20 **Listen and write the words.** Then go to page 80. TR: 8.21

1. _ _ _ _ _
   12

2. _ _ _ _ _ _ _
   15 10 6 13

3. _ _ _ _ _ _
   17 2

4. _ _ _ _ _ _
   4

1 **Listen.** Then listen and repeat. TR: 9.1 and 9.2

silent
gh

silent
w

1.

2.

ei**gh**t   dou**gh**nut

1.

2.

write   t**w**o

2 **Trace and say.**

3 **Listen.** Circle the words with a silent *gh*. TR: 9.3

1. laugh   2. neighbour   3. ghost   4. daughter

4 **Listen and repeat.** Put the letters in order to make words. TR: 9.4

1.    2.    3.    4.

_____   _____   _____   _____
wrdso   itlhg   rpwa   hegwi

5 **Listen.** Then listen and repeat. TR: 9.5 and 9.6

sure

1.

2.

treasure   measure

ture

1.

2.

nature   picture

6 **Trace and say.**

7 **Can you hear a word with sure or ture?** Listen and write the number *1–4*. TR: 9.7

sure ☐ ☐   ture ☐ ☐

8 **Can you hear sure or ture?** Listen and write. TR: 9.8

1.

2.

3.

4.

sculp＿＿＿   vul＿＿＿   furni＿＿＿   enclo＿＿＿

9 **Listen to the rhyming words.** Then listen and repeat.
TR: 9.9 and 9.10

goat

train

money

coat

plane

honey

10 **Read the rhyming words.**

11 **Do the words rhyme?** Listen and circle *Yes* or *No.* TR: 9.11

I. Yes No   2. Yes No   3. Yes No   4. Yes No

12 **Listen and repeat.** Circle all the words that rhyme. TR: 9.12

I.    2.    3.    4.

13 **Listen to the words that sound the same.** Then listen and repeat. TR: 9.13 and 9.14

one

road

pair

won

rode

pear

14 **Read the words that sound the same.**

15 **Listen.** Circle the word pairs that sound the same. TR: 9.15

1. meet, meat   2. read, red   3. hear, hair   4. wait, weight

16 **Listen and repeat.** Put the letters in order to make words. TR: 9.16

1.

2.

3.

4.

_____   _____   _____   _____
   lufor   lwfroe   tihrg   ertwi

67

17 **Follow the path to the sounds.** Write the words. Then listen and check. TR: 9.17

1. -ture

2. silent *gh*

3. *sunny* rhymes with...

4. *by* sounds like...

1. _____

_____

2. _____

_____

3. _____

_____

4. _____

_____

18 **Listen.** Then listen and chant. TR: 9.18

It's the weekend! Hooray!
There's no school today!
We can stay at home
or go outside and play!

The museum was an adventure.
We saw lots of old treasure.
The mummies were wrapped up tight.
They gave my sister quite a fright.

It's the weekend! Hooray!
There's no school today!
We can stay at home
or go outside and play!

19 **Listen.** Then listen and repeat. TR: 9.19 and 9.20

Aunt Elena and the Ants

Pedro and his aunt and uncle went on a nature adventure.

Look! There are bees in those trees!

They rode horses on a road. They heard a strange noise.

It's a herd of cows!

They had snacks in their backpacks. Doughnuts!

Delightful!

We ate eight!

Look, Aunt Elena, a big ant!

What's wrong?

Eek! Ants on my hands!

20 **Listen and write the words.** Then go to page 80. TR: 9.21

1. __ __ __ __ __
   14 7

2. __ __ __ __ __
   16 10

3. __ __ __ __ __
   18 8

4. __ __ __ __ __
   17 2

Review

1 Work in pairs. Put the letters in order to make words.

iybtardh

b_____ y

_____

Move forwards I space.

nniioivatt

i_____ n

neke

k_____

Start

_____

_____

pigsnr

s_____

_____

70

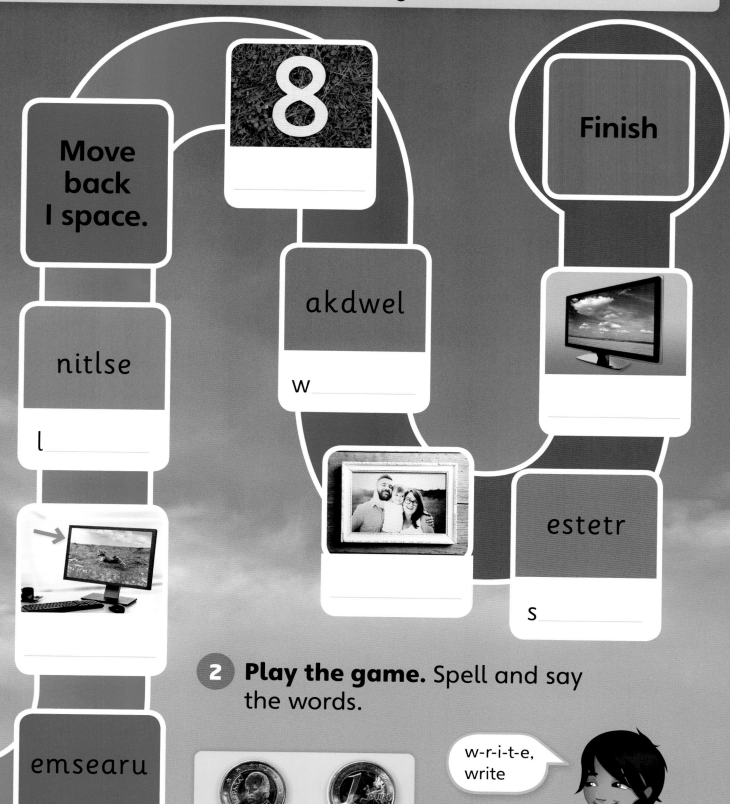

silent t tion sion ed th d silent gh silent w sure ture

8

Move back 1 space.

akdwel

w_____

Finish

nitlse

l_____

estetr

s_____

emsearu

m_____e

2 **Play the game.** Spell and say the words.

Heads: Move 1 space.

Tail: Move 2 spaces.

w-r-i-t-e, write

Picture Dictionary

1   a/e/i/o/u   er/or/our   air/are/ear

2   ar   or   ear/eer   ir/ear/er

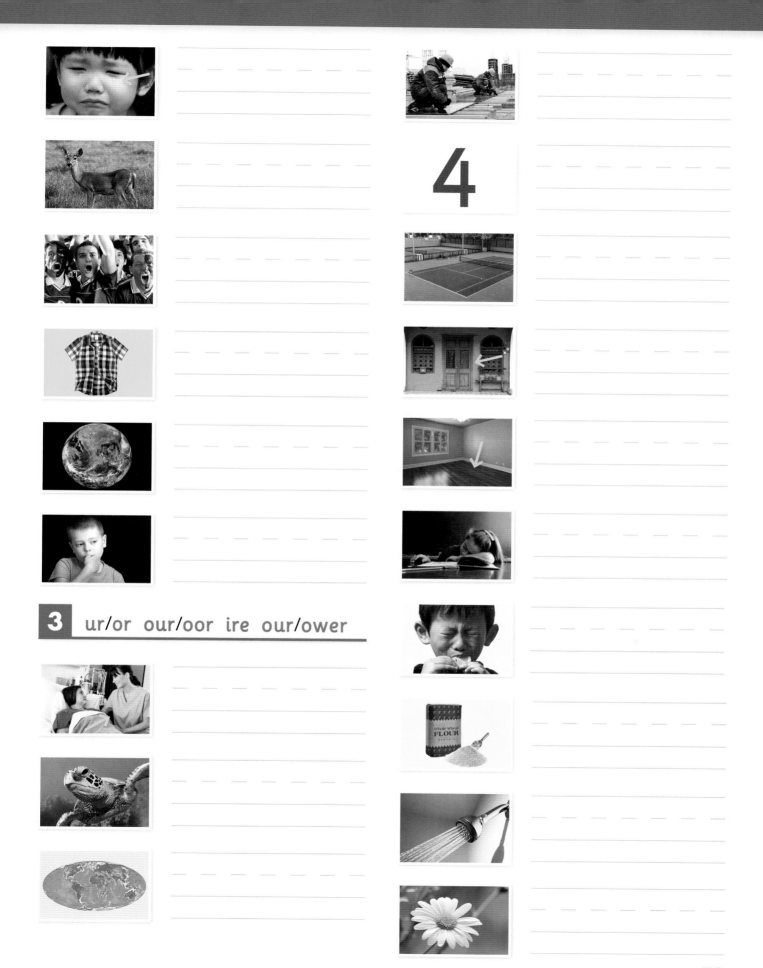

3 ur/or our/oor ire our/ower

4 s, s, es   ful, ous   qu, squ
f/ph/gh

5 nd, nk, nt   g, g   silent d,
silent h nch, rch

74

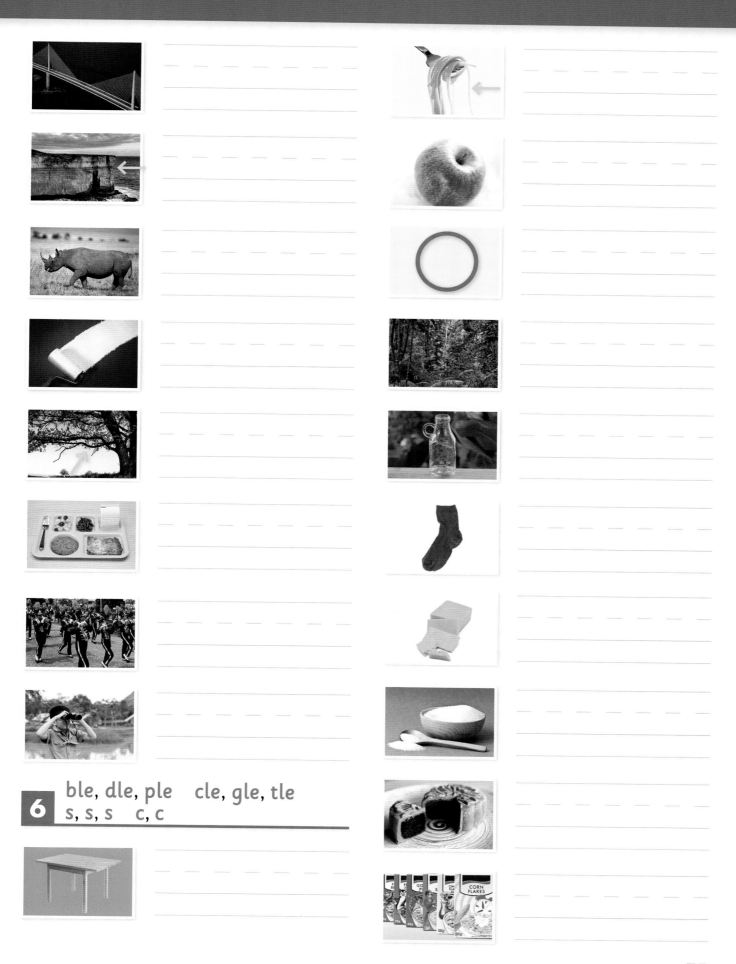

6   ble, dle, ple   cle, gle, tle
    s, s, s   c, c

7 spr, spl str, scr shr, thr silent k, silent t

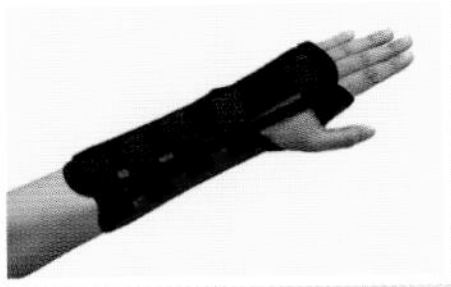

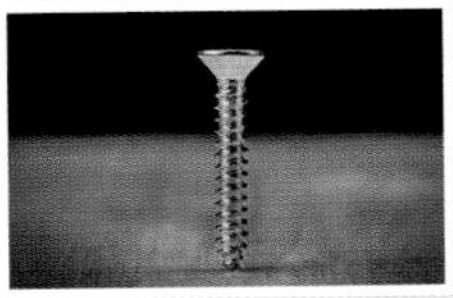

8 tion, sion ed, ed, ed th, th, d

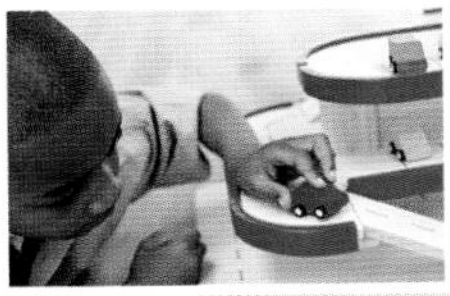

silent **gh**, silent **w**   **sure**, **ture**
rhyming, same sounds (homophones)

Write the letters from Activity 20 in the box. Then use the code to write the words. Read the sentence.

Unit 1
(page 17)

s		m	n	d	p		l
1	2	3	4	5	6	7	8
	k	t		f	g		h
9	10	11	12	13	14	15	16

__ __ __ __ __ __ __ ,   __ __ __ __ __ __   __ __ __ __ __   __ __ __ __ __
7　4　14　2　8　12　1　　1　9　1　11　2　15　　3　7　10　2　1　　1　7　8　7　5

__ __ __　__ __ __　__ __ __ __ __ __ .
13　12　15　　11　16　2　　6　7　15　15　12　11

Unit 2
(page 23)

p		f	h	k		y	b	
1	2	3	4	5	6	7	8	9
u		t	n	s	d		m	c
10	11	12	13	14	15	16	17	18

__ __ __ __ __ __ __ __　__ __ __ __　__　T- __ __ __ __ __　__ __ __
3　11　2　13　6　13　15　6　　8　10　7　14　　6　　14　4　16　2　12　　6　12　6

__ __ __ __　__ __ __ __　__ __ __　__ __ __ __ .
14　4　9　1　　13　11　6　2　　12　4　11　　1　6　2　5

Unit 3
(page 29)

p		n	s	k		t	
1	2	3	4	5	6	7	8
l	a	h			f	m	
9	10	11	12	13	14	15	16

__ __ __　C __ __ __　__ __ __ __ __　__ __ __　__ __ __ __ __ __ __　b _ g
15　16　4　　11　8　3　　4　11　2　1　4　　14　2　16　　10　1　12　16　1　9　8　　10

__ __　__ __ __　__ __ __ __ __ __　__ __ __ __　__ __　__ __ __ __ .
2　3　　7　11　8　　14　2　12　16　7　11　　14　9　2　2　16　　2　14　　10　4　11　2　1

Write the letters from Activity 20 in the box. Then use the code to write the words. Read the sentence.

Unit 4
(page 37)

___	k	___	___	n	d	i	___	r
1	2	3	4	5	6	7	8	9

a	m	___	t	o	e	c	___	___
10	11	12	13	14	15	16	17	18

___ ___ ___ ___ ___ ,   ___ ___ ___ ___ ___ ___ ___   ___ ___ ___   ___ ___ ___ ___ ___ ___ ___
1 10 13 15 9   12 15 1 7 16 7 10   10 5 6   8 13 15 17 3 15 5

___ ___ ___ ___   ___   ___ ___ ___ ___ ___ ___ ___   ___ ___ ___ ___ ___ ___   ___ ___ ___ ___ .
11 10 2 15   10   6 15 1 7 16 7 14 4 8   8 18 4 10 8 3   16 10 2 15

Unit 5
(page 43)

f	i	w	l	___	___	p	___	___	y
1	2	3	4	5	6	7	8	9	10

k	a	___	u	___	o	e	s	b	d
11	12	13	14	15	16	17	18	19	20

___ ___ ___   ___ ___ ___ ___ ___   ___ ___ ___ ___   ___ ___ ___ ___ ___   ___ ___ ___
6 13 17   8 2 5 4 18   7 2 15 11   3 13 2 6 17   12 9 20

___ ___ ___ ___ ___ ___   ___ ___ ___ ___ ___ ___   ___ ___   ___ ___ ___   ___ ___ ___ ___ .
16 5 12 9 8 17   1 4 16 3 17 5 18   19 10   6 13 17   7 16 9 20

Unit 6
(page 49)

___	k	d	___	t	a	___	i	w
1	2	3	4	5	6	7	8	9

h	___	u	y	r	b	n	___	o
10	11	12	13	14	15	16	17	18

___ ___ ___ ___ ___   ___ ___ ___   ___ ___ ___   ___ ___ ___ ___ ___   ___ ___ ___ ___
17 1 11 6 14   6 16 3   10 8 11   12 16 17 7 1   14 8 3 1

___ ___ ___ ___ ___ ___   ___ ___ ___ ___ ___ ___ ___ ___   ___ ___   ___ ___ ___   ___ ___ ___ ___ ___ ___ .
4 12 14 4 7 1   15 8 17 13 17 7 1 11   5 18   15 12 13   17 10 1 1 11 1

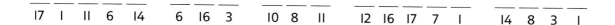

Write the letters from Activity 20 in the box. Then use the code to write the words. Read the sentence.

Unit 7
(page 57)

1	2	3	4	5	6	7	8	9
___	d	n	c	e	___	b	m	___

10	11	12	13	14	15	16	17	18
x	___	w	a	h	___	i	___	o

___ ___ ___ ___   ___ ___ ___ ___   ___ ___ ___ ___ ___   ___   ___ ___ ___ ___ ___ ___
15 3 18 10   8 13 2 5   8 16 11 4 14   13   7 13 3 13 3 13

___ ___ ___ ___ ___   ___ ___ ___ ___   ___ ___ ___ ___ ___ ___ ___ ___ ___ .
1 9 17 16 11   12 16 11 14   1 9 6 16 3 15 17 5 1

Unit 8
(page 63)

1	2	3	4	5	6	7	8	9
u	___	c	___	v	___	l	r	f

10	11	12	13	14	15	16	17	18
___	b	___	___	w	___	a	___	y

,

___ ___ ___ ___ ___   ___   ___ ___ ___ ___ ___ ___ ___   ___ ___ ___ ___ ___ ___ ___
4 16 10 18 1   15   11 8 6 17 2 12 8   14 16 17 3 2 12 4

___ ___ ___ ___ ___ ___ ___ ___ ___ ___   ___ ___ ___ ___ ___   ___ ___ ___   ___ ___ ___ ___ ___ ___ ___ ___ ___ ___ ___ .
17 12 7 12 5 10 15 10 6 13   16 9 17 12 8   17 2 12   3 12 7 12 11 8 16 17 10 6 13

Unit 9
(page 69)

1	2	3	4	5	6	7	8	9
o	___	s	v	d	n	___	___	i

10	11	12	13	14	15	16	17	18
___	b	p	m	___	l	___	___	___

___ ___ ___ ___ ___   ___ ___ ___ ___ ___   ___ ___ ___   ___ ___ ___ ___ ___ ___   ___ ___
12 17 5 10 1   16 10 1 14 17   14 16 1   17 13 2 9 15 3   14 1

___ ___ ___   ___ ___ ___   ___ ___ ___ ___ ___   ___ ___ ___   ___ ___ ___ ___ ___ ___ ___ ___ ___ .
8 9 3   13 7 13   2 11 1 7 14   8 9 3   2 5 4 17 6 14 7 10 17

80